SAFETY RAZOR

Emily Osborne

Guelph, Ontario

Edited by Shane Neilson
Cover and book design by Jeremy Luke Hill
Proofreading by Carol Dilworth
Set in Linux Libertine
Printed on Mohawk Via Felt
Printed and bound by Arkay Design & Print

LIBRARY AND ARCHIVES CANADA CATALOGUING IN PUBLICATION

Title: Safety razor / Emily Osborne.
Names: Osborne, Emily (Poet), author.
Description: Poems.
Identifiers: Canadiana (print) 20220481040 | Canadiana (ebook)
    20220481091 | ISBN 9781774220856 (softcover) |
    ISBN 9781774220863 (PDF) | ISBN 9781774220870 (EPUB)
Classification: LCC PS8629.S36 S24 2023 | DDC C811/.6—dc23

Gordon Hill Press gratefully acknowledges the support of the Canada Council for the Arts, the Ontario Arts Council, and the Ontario Book Tax Publishing Credit.

Gordon Hill Press respectfully acknowledges the ancestral homelands of the Attawandaron, Anishinaabe, Haudenosaunee, and Métis Peoples, and recognizes that we are situated on Treaty 3 territory, the traditional territory of Mississaugas of the Credit First Nation.

Gordon Hill Press also recognizes and supports the diverse persons who make up its community, regardless of race, age, culture, ability, ethnicity, nationality, gender identity and expression, sexual orientation, marital status, religious affiliation, and socioeconomic status.

Gordon Hill Press
130 Dublin Street North
Guelph, Ontario, Canada
N1H 4N4
www.gordonhillpress.com

Table of Contents

III: FLESH MEETS

For Daniel

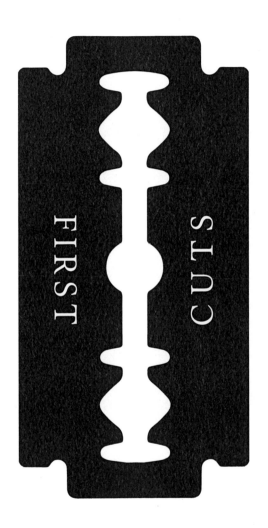

FIRST CUTS

Infant amnesia

Thunder strums through my earliest memory
of family dinner. Summer in Ontario,

lightning pulses on the table. In the post-
voltaic hush, Dad tunes the radio to sirens,

tornado. We rush to the basement but
I'm leashed to my highchair so Dad hauls

the hybrid downstairs, my bib scattering
remnants in the dim. Sarah hugs her cabbage

patch kid, asks if the house will pop off us
like a lid. Matt jumps a vigil at the high slit

of window while hailstones pelt, clouds cutting
their diamond lumps. Mum finds me a bunny.

Don't worry. I don't remember fear, only
us here in its eye. If the radio wheezed *safety*,

it's blurry. Can amygdalae bind memory
so early? Does terror find us in utero?

Trauma soaking the placenta like lightning
charging soil with nitrogen. Maybe I'm wrong,

maybe amnesia begins in our concrete shell:
growling for the winds to let us out, buckling

when our house twists to rubble in the angry
                                           funnel.

Before I'm supposed to remember, maybe we
emerged not to resume dinner, drawn closer

by false alarms, but to meet these chance wrecks,
lives torn apart before we're pieced together.

Sometimes I glimpse this error in my cortex,
in the grip or quiver of my mother's arms.

Decepticon

Plastic assassin, a twist-snap
transformer hiding handguns,
annihilating blobs in corners.

He senses plots rattling behind
doorknobs, resents nights when
he is Tetrused in a box between

wooden blocks and the polyester
bear. Free tonight, his saw-toothed
boots stump the rug, passing

the athlete with trademark cap
and swing. He knows there's
an order to all created things.

In the corner, open-palmed Jesus
molded in robes, passionless through
tantrums. But Decepticon hasn't got ears,

can't hear what all that means.
He's seen machines, some unfolding
and flashing chromatic screens

and wants to know why his chest
has a sticker, icon only glowing
at the rub of a child's finger.

Urban planning

Sister, do you remember how we played
alone together in summer-charred
suburbs? Shooed out for fresh air when
other kids lolled by AC units and Sega.

How tarmac rasped our nostrils like a match
until we made games from shade patches,
switch-backed through sprinklers, knife-sharp
mouths spitting cool diamonds on our flesh.

How jump ropes cut caked air, PVC's
live wire cocooning us before it
lashed our calves. Sister, there were plastic
snakes in summer. So we roamed wider—

found hopscotch etched on concrete heat,
squares like neon flour on a counter
after pans were chucked in the oven.
Some kids had strict parents, were called

inside for dinner. Did I give you
a bandaid when you fell on train tracks,
your blood lumpy with black nail grease?
My pockets were empty. How many

abandoned yards, old cemeteries
were scouted before we noticed thirst?
Somehow summer was inside us, a dry
failure to swallow, like we'd opened

our mouths serpentine for ripe spoils
far bigger than our two slight bodies.

Venn diagrams

In school we group foods into circles:
      write here the epithelium's ripe plums
write here rhubarb puckers   rinds citrus-stung
      write here glutamate of muscle
chloride pep of pretzels.   In the rings' overlap
write flavours that cross ion channels
      that sweet-salt glut of peanut butter,
mouth stuck through lunch
            alone at a round table.
That sucrose rush from recess, my gobstoppers
      swiped by bigger fists
        shellacked with citric acid
   Tag, you're it
      don't panic, just run in circles.
         Saliva acrid through music,
my flute's embouchure high with rubbing alcohol
      and tarnish.
         A caesura missed
conductor signing
   the winds aren't in sync.
         Chalk, zinc, the flavours of math,
licking pastel gypsum from my thumb
      botching formulas before the whole class
   someone else knows it's a sum plus a sum
galvanic prick of graphite when I suck
      my pencil, hide my head at my desk
   and scribble coils
      remember the sharp gun-metal
of an adult's tongue on mine.
      Some tastes you can't categorize.

Home for supper, mum spoons up
      ham-and-potato pabulum
bland pan smelling of *our debts don't level.*
   Still we say prayers prescriptive as pills,
with milk to swill and glue to swallow.

Dad foretells our lives with diagrams
but mum's not eating
            you're speaking in circles.

Before bed, I brush my mouth piquant
            and spit mint, spit mint
                toxic if ingested
in the mirror   spy my epiglottis raw with tiny dots
and two rusting ovals
            where I bit my cheeks to iron.

Now I lay me down
                with canker sores
        a stung palate
                I pray the lord
my teacher said
you'll savour less bitter when you're older
                give me what's sweet
            my soul to keep
let me taste
            before I wake
a little less young
            my soul to take
my unbled tongue

Sharp parables

Children hear of water-hoardings.
Lorelei floating gold cups, coaxing
gullible girls down. Ancient cities
settled by kelp and shells.
Rivers refusing tossed-in shoes,
certain that boys thought dead
are somewhere still, walking.

So we puzzled our lake
with threadbare toys, scraps
and warpings, watching swells
lull, and shellac our discards.

In winter we moved whisper-dust
rumours, of wakes under deep
prison glass, the lake's keeping,
where the missing swam with
objects we once owned.

Officials would come,
piecing past a lacustrine spot,
with stop-walk reports:
there, the forest tarping
white-ambered tracks;
there, slumped trees
shouldering cuffs of wind;
there, a hut tired of
hearth-stories, rough nights
charred by tree-cuttings—

Cold shapes inhabit fables:
winter father, cooling daughters,
a queen's snow-spool unraveling,
tales of caution restless, gathering.
A child's body, riddled with ice-shards,
and growing numb on endless games.

By spring, our eyes are fogged
and frost-buckled, mirroring
only parables sharp and bleak.
Through cracks, we see a lake
brimming with a lost brother.

"Auðr mourns her dead brother"

Sorrow, laughter's slayer, forces
from the lady a wave of tears.
Water-fruits drip from the fair forest
of her eyelids, pool in her lap.
The goddess of the serpent's gold bed
gleans those drupes from woe-bloated
eyes, plucks them from hazel lashes
and pines for me, the Óðinn of praise.

This gold-goddess slides her limbs
under linen, but sleep is not
there. Tears drip from swollen eyes,
the brine-bowls of dreams.
On her cheeks, the thrones of eyes,
tears are trapped. The stately oak-tree
collects this dew which dispels
peace, all for her dead brother.

I dream in falling motion

not midair abandon, but skirred
surfaces. Sled magnetic to snow,
shearing trunks and barbed fences.
Our gear-jammed van skidding

through clogged cities—late, late
as always. Red wagon on hot
concrete, my sister's hair whip-fine
and blinding, hands noosing the stiff handle.

When I find footholds, morning always
calls it sleepwalking. Shelves hollow,
clothes dumped in bundles like the shells
                          of raptured children.

Sisyphus could stop, turn, roll
his ball-and-chain uphill again.
There's some hope, in pushing stalled
millstones up slopes.

Here is without impact, no saved soul
lifts from kinked metal.

Samhain song

After the first purchased costumes,
soon outgrown, our mother told us
to make our own. Such skills
we lacked. We plundered her closet

for reject threads: black sack dress paired
with paper witch's cap, peasant blouse
with peace signs on foreheads.
From a back recess, grandma's nurse corps

uniform. Soon there was war:
not razored sugar or bullies' tricks,
but air sharp to narrow ribs, taffy
pulling a loose baby tooth in a gush

of bloodied root, hands blued round
plastic pumpkins of goods, bare legs
inflamed from the earth's quarter tilt.
At ten I carried grandfather's cross

and chalice, my sister playing the sick
congregant he salved on home visits.
Who did we appease that one night
given us to roam free? We spirits

were hungry ghosts of Samhain satisfied
by offerings, yet we returned no favours,
gave no protection through winter.
Sister, tell me, did we abuse our ancestors

by making them costumes? Home was cursed,
our father chronic with fever, hands swollen,
hauling burdens through cold. We sorted
sweet hoardings, brought him favoured portions.

Yet his father, his shrouded
power, stayed buried with their blessings.

Twin paradox

Her mother, too rotund with child,
must have guessed
                  a second coming.
The twin an unplanned pic—
                          misty, squished.

As a kid, she knew her twin hid
in crowds, left snack-wraps
and socks as clues in playgrounds.

        Not mirror imaged.
Both have teal irises, tined teeth, criss-cross scars
on left feet.
                But her twin's cinematic
                      in Lycra or Crocs.
                When she glosses full lips
                                no one asks
if she likes thick cocks.
She never labels thoughts dirty,
                      spikes coffee with vodka,
                                        happily.

Her twin lives where time outfoxes
photoshop and Botox,
                spackling brows,
                spindling sin with a beautician's needle.
Regret's optional, an analog clock
                        no one checks.
She clicks *yes*, inviting the stranger.

                        It's lunch.
Then she plucks gooey grapes from Ziploc,
thighs aromatic.

When time circles back
it won't be traumatic. Her twin
was not brought up on Pentecostal preaching,
            does not feel guilty

for backsliding.

                    She imagines the Second Coming—
        dazzling sky-rift and trumpets,
        throngs identical buoyed above
                    the blueberry-runt Earth.

A cloud screen replays buried scenes
to the damned: backlit thoughts,
                    lions fornicating with lambs.

When Christ cues her reel

                    it's divine—

the bit where she fingers herself in a mirror
        lips
        peach cheekbones
            slits

                    in a crucifix.

The camera shifts to the ménage á trois,
        an unknown hand
                unhooks her bra—
                    man or spirit?
wet breath in her ear,
        I've counted the hairs on your head

                            ah ha

Shared kitchen

Three minutes hum, electromagnetic.
Dinner splutters on its plastic cover,
mashed foods groomed to nuke in sync.
She peels scorched film, recalls mums

cursing fast menus, warped tools—
Here's a balanced meal, grace, a drink.
She debates the rimmed
tray, nice plates, won't risk spills in loaned

rooms.
                                There's
gardens
she's never used, but hunger's unblunted
by backyard blooms.
                        Convenience aisles
cut chitchat in shared kitchens, time on dials.

Her window's sealed shut,
                        but it has a view:
city like a child, fuelled by the nine-to-six.
Give thanks for the microwave's quick
fix, for eating solo,
                  maybe for two.

Wendy Bird

At the stage-set window in the local
theatre, the Wendy Bird perches every
evening, crying *Peter! Peter!* In eggshell-
blue nightgown, under gold yolks of light
spilling from the rafters, she's pre-pubescent,
though really thirty. Slight bird piping

to the darkness, she glues the boy's nylon
shadow, floats pathosward when her bound
breast's arrowed, mimes horror while Hook
and Peter boss out wit and wooden swords.
But *Crowds lack focus*, the director shrugs,
snipping her script with shoulders up.

There's the rub. She flubbed her job
at drama camp, let squirts carouse
and ditch their parts to hit each other
with sticks. Asked to serve up lunch,
she masked her morning sick with crackers
pinched from the tweedling mob. Mums

say *Motherhood's the toughest job*,
though Wendy notes *Most females do it.*
Hiding a six-month bump is rough even
under loose pyjamas. Soon she'll mind
small objects: breast pump, bright pink
sippy cup, pastel fabrics clustered in a nest.

She'll lay down daughter's daughters, girls
who slip away from youth in pirate ships,
slim legs trailing see-through silks. A Jane-
bird parts lips to sky, learns to cry *Peter!*
She'll feign spring cleaning for babytooth boys,
hiding tattooed sparrows on her thigh.

In the pantry

Cans batched by date and contents,
arranged   just-not   touching.

Like replicas of retro art
of mass production.

Like flash card animals
flipped to match
their cartoon mates.

The back-row tomatoes'
rust-gibbous lid plugged
                with slow poison.

Might this metal rip in landfills,
ooze stew in toothsome TV-ad red?

How vivid the unseen, the
                puncture
of the can opener's
                merry-go-round teeth.
Only a wrist flick,
                and what-ifs spin closer,
like acrylic chromed horses,
                a jingle over-encored,
a girl's tug at mother's pliant hand
                to ride the open-eyed colts
again, again.

Revisiting

Our bridge home mortars
the broken wrist of water
in air and earth—a prosthetic
gesture. From here, our road
seams like a frayed gravel skein,
and home is a wooden knot
the width of my closed fist.

Apologies we've shifted,
like sand held in an houred
hollow with a rust of patience;
but each visit we've overstepped.

In retrospect, the way back's unkept,
and though I parse my breath in tandem
(treading an Odyssean pace), this
re-run road needs a porch light's grace.

In gratitude for arriving, our
door loses its latitude, unhandled
as a bone ajar, severed
at a knuckle's beating

(these are words for welcome,
tokens, like a host retreating)

but in the bare ache of greeting,
our arms are unlike a simile,
when proximity brings careful parallels
to breaking points of possibility

"Sonatorrek"

Hardly can I hoist
my tongue or mount
song's steelyard, forge verse
in my mind's foundry.

My tear-sea swamps
poetry, yet verse flows
like gore from a giant's
throat onto Hel's port.

The cruel sea hacked through
the fence of my kin.
A gap rots, unfilled,
where my sons flourished.

I carried one son's corpse.
I carry word-timber,
leafed in language,
from the speech-shrine.

Antarctic Anthem

White Rorschach from a satellite, in your igneous platforms
and sheepback rocks we see strange shapes. Chipped marble.
Asymmetric brain. Popcorn kernel. Deflating balloon zooming
through blue air. Vulnerably in vogue. In the Equinox Sale
I bought a frost-hued top with glacial drapes, ice-cap appliqués,
trousers arête-stitched. The Antarctic Look, touted as the antidote
to cyclical fashion, to blogs swapping neutrals with neons.
Your skyline's been styled the same for eons. Sure, I've hunted
frozen youth down cosmetic aisles, spackled wrinkles with anemone-
cell cream. Had conscious brunch of *penguin egg pancakes* made
from lichen, quenched hangovers with *arctic milk* from a Kelvin-
scale machine. Tithes from my meal conserve your cryosphere's
thin-skinned sheen. Friends and I have opposed kayak tourism,
hosted darkness retreats to detox from light pollution, raced to raise
study-money for the polar vortex. Gone further. Tried hits of *diamond
dust*, one rough-edged drug—conjures the aurora australis, frostnips
cheeks with tattle-tale blisters. We've wept *terror* and *erebus* when
our vision double-dutched. One uncut winter, we wrote this anthem:

> *From darkest aphelion to shining perihelion,*
> *from mounts Ellsworth to Vinson—*

but we scrapped that start. Tried again.

> *We see your gleaming shores,*
> *on which no wars were fought;*
> *where treaties guard the seas,*
> *where climate change is fraught—*

That quatrain was idiotic, but stay with me,
this is the best part:

> *O Antarctica, white myth from antiquity,*
> *continent unstung by blood, wait for us while*
> *this mucky atmosphere heats up. We'll be*
> *your pioneers after the world-wide flood.*

Goddesses marooned on your denuded rocks,
sewing clothes from hair grass and gems,
munching magenta starfish for breakfast.
Generations will call us blessed.

Only we will know which lakes hold microbes
proving life on Jupiter's Europa, the safe
places to entomb earth's nuclear waste.
Diplomats will send us thanks:

pears from Asia's last gardens,
marrow from Africa's last steppes.
Then they'll rocket away from this dystopia.
From deep space they'll spot us in telescopes,

right under the auroral chrome.
Land so reflective it makes artists
jealous. They've seen it all now,
the greatest human—earth schism—

but who can paint us? A little cracked
opal, pulsing in a plasma screen's prism.

Glassblowing

Fill my cupboard-cool glass, just a little red pool
before going out. They say this freeze will snap.
Feedback currents will roll, street ice and global floes
crinkle back like shrink wrap. Am I almost ready,

just dressing by the wood stove's glory hole?
We'll risk the cold, winter cap clasping Murano
spheres to earlobes, jewels cryogenic on skin.
For months we've seen that smelt sky cloned,

town blurred in talcum snow unless we chrome
our photos. You guide my numb elbow through
doors, out of coats, to soirées interglacial, throats
tepid with talk, champagne staid to palms. The only jolt?

Flutes fractured as I've lost you. A stranger raises
cheers—his corneas like camera lenses, milk-blue sclera
edged in red. Orbs foreign as planets frozen,
then fissured to capillaries. And he drones on—

did you know earth wobbles in orbit, that
Greenland's ice cores were filled with carbon
bubbles, that we're in another Ice Age,
a tipsy ellipse?

It's almost tomorrow. You and I slip
out, watch people coil through windows, buildings
hued like Reticello bottles. Our voices muted
by tuques, only the sirens' garnet whine. Streets over,

glass has shattered like a chilled cup brimming
with hot liquid—carelessness burst to bone-stubs
in a bloodshot slide. So are our eyes, slit against
mint air. Carpe noctem, with mittened fists we spin

around lamp-posts blown out to kindled ornaments,
for a moment acrobats, drunk on what's solid
or bound to crack. Tomorrow, snow will clench to cubes,
clink down rivers like iced drinks, tumblers

nursed after arguments. Tomorrow we'll search
photos, phones flipping friends with strangers.
In colour, we're together, frozen, passed,
like all the fluid things we've seen through glass.

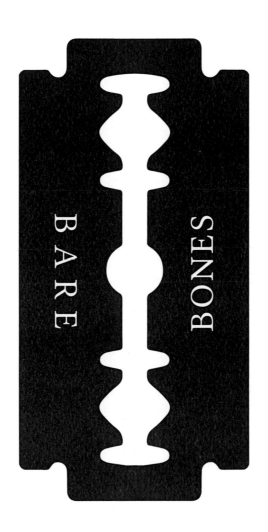

"Verse making"

Goddess of the rune-carved mead mug,
I've smoothed the prow of this song-ship.
Lovely lady, tree who carries cups,
I deftly ply my tongue, the lathe of poems.

Scrimshaw

Sails wheel the atoll,
white teeth clench
on a volcanic clot.

On deck, the scrimshander culls
a tusk, his needle pricking baleen
with breakers and peaks.
Pin dipped in tobacco spit,
he inks mountains, tracing basalt
that once rasped the slopes and
blistered sand to black.

A scab, this island,
re-bled through vents until
it puckered above water.
Tattooed onto dentin by whalers
whittling hours after hunts,
when mammoths slit the surface,
when blood thinned to aqua and salt,
and whales' pulsed calls
thumped the ship's hull.

To finish the tooth, he'll onyx it
with candle soot and file off its roots.

Art opens from wounds as far back
as anyone dates it. Death lays down
a flat canvas for carving.

Art is younger than dirt, only
as old as petroglyphs coating
earth's aortas; only as old as
carbon in caves, as stencilled
hands that hunted animals
until they were food,
or painted, or tabooed.

Dinosaur bones

A six-foot femur and two ulnas
cemented in clay spell "k."
Once an abc body, now a crabbed
Akkadian on cracked tablets.

Gloved hands have reglued and displayed
them as clues of cannibal diets
and ash disasters.

Victorians gave them reptile flesh,
fit for Crystal Palaces. Ladies laced
in whalebone gazed at slick green
haunches, traded postcards where they bathed
in watercolour arcadias.

Now we know they were brutal birds,
pack-hunters who pecked gullets
before they burned.

Still, they're plush-toy gold,
Ice Age goofs,
or house-trained in cartoons.

I've written letters on violent
memories, wiped them clean
for flaunting on the internet.
Some are cute. Some I've made
fleshy and feathered for this post-
porn generation, kissable as glass
in glass cases.

"Rune carving"

Bench-fellow, you've brewed beer-curses,
cloaking cunning in these horns.
But you've miss-stepped in your sport,
for I carve runes on the mead-cups,
sealing word-play with bright blood.
Secret signs I locked on this horn,
this tree-root of the wild beast's ears.
How will the swamp-malt swell in us?

Ale eddies me, but it blenches my
bench-mate. Rain from the ox's horn
drenches my beard. Your wit's downright
brainlessness, bench-fellow. Warrior,
you hold ale like a wimp, although you
scatter spear-showers to scour shields.
From my mouth poetry pours.
Óðinn's rain overwhelms everyone.

Diacritics

Maybe all vowels were once sister chromatids,
but now we carve grave and caret on separate
word trees. *I can't read your DNA or lips.*

You said my consonants split and replicate
like cells in tumours. Writing them makes
you stressed? Possessives are tricky on paper,

so often inked with red. After classes, ESL
students roam cities, see kids slash 'ł' and 'ø'
on concrete artistry. *Is that Polish? No.*

Paint bleeds. Later they'll sit at library PCs
typing home without familiar glyphs.
Viewpoints online metastasize through hashtag

alphabets, while English pushes diacritics
out of foreign correspondence. Keyboards
are capricious, and we're étroit d'esprit

when small things make big shifts.
Hardly anybody knows if these are those
when articles sound like blips, clitics

slipped from a stranger's tongue.
*I don't care who's Pooh or Piglet, use
my words when you play at my house.*

Tonight, who gambles with commas,
decimals? We all lose track of cash.
Few know how Gauss advanced

the abcs of polynomials, how numbers
hail in a global dialect. *Is that Unicode? No.*
Dead keys release mutations the more

we upload symbols. For a discourse
universal, I'd mock-up binary signs,
word combos that (=) or (≠).

Is that fascist? No. It's abstract logic,
the zone where sentences always
yield satisfactions.

Relativity of simultaneity

The train is punctual in its glossy enamel.
The train auto-corrects, inserting commas
into a run-on sentence. In these caesuras,
doors open in sync to greet commuters.

Or do they? I'm running along the platform,
but the nearest door is always closing sooner.
The train's line scans in iambic metre, lips
contracting one syllable after another.

Smoked out

Offhand we burn offense, when we're out of town routines, ignoring trail arrows and altitudes for composure, breeding smoke squalls in forests, choking our eyes. *Back down.* Evening glare flags park hours and protocols for ceding. We make the gate, but your warning kept pace, lipped with a light.

Back home. After work, second-hand pressure draws minutes through throat and fingers. You float questions: crabbed clouds scratching at the window catching—someone has to vent this stalemate. Down steel-drum stairs, curbed by night, crooked sidewalk squares, your appetite for ash escorting me like an obiter dictum; wafted, free.

Cordoned with alleys, dawn notches past roofs; an aubade of pipes and heaters trips my out-of-bed alarm. *Hang on.* Strangers offer coffee, sunrise scalds muscles from sleep. Street signs make fickle quips, that trail ends and evacuation routes won't loop home; each road barbed with block letters.

Thunderclap

Two hemispheres pressure each other,
heat bullying gray-cold matter.

Chill air contracts a pyrexic afternoon,
cumulating static from human pollution

and the displeasure of divinities,
who discard electric weapons
casually, charging supercells
and insecurities in our nerves
as we wait out this storm,
stalled in our car.

We can never predict the triggers.

The brontide throbs the dash
before the sky zippers. Black teeth
unclaw from bright gashes when I blink—

Twice I packed my handbag,
but this aspirin has expired.

The windshield blurs in aura
and the nausea of sodden earth
seeps through rubber cracks.
Cars should have almanacs
for cranial pain,
radars for bitter weather,
counters for thunderclaps.

Squabbles crowd our blind spots
with airbag haste. Stratus cusping
through windows unvalved—words
foul the glass and can't evaporate.

Weather forecasting

Ancients knew planets threw anvils
into clouds, released cold rains

and chilblains. Gods hissed ice pellets,
until farmers hid indoors for weeks,

sealing windows in blubber and rusted
blood. Souls lost in blizzards watched

them sup bad water and reread the prophets.
From a cell's screen a man knows how long

he has to walk the dog, before red pixels
blot out the province. While doggie squats

on unguarded lawns, he watches neighbours
glaze TV, omens snug in ultra-sharp HD.

His globe is meshed in electric fence,
whirring with what's coming. It sees

meteors thrown from ether. But a man
can't see with god-eyes the weather forming,

far-off pressure banking, molding moisture
to tornados, a silver-purple chalice pouring

wrath on grasslands. As evening indigos,
he throws to doggie a blink-jingling ball.

What signs are in the beasts, in heaven?
Even ancients knew before thunder the dog

hides its tail like a snuffed-out comet.

JUMBO

How far back stretch the facts elephants
never forget? To their kindergarten years
suckling in savannahs? To your fifth
summer and your mother, her last trump

at the cards of hunters? Your new fear
of man's face, his reedy finger cupping
a trigger the size and shade of your toe?
O Jumbo, how much you've grown

crossing to Suez and Europe, London Zoo
and Barnum's show. In metres, almost four.
You've shed scabs you wore in Paris cages.
London brings endless buns to eat, wages

from tots with tuppence. Does bread taste
sweet as Sudan's molasses grass? With those
great ears, flapping like a sail's slack to the wind
of words, have you learned English?

Children know your gleaming eyes wear
sympathy, your gentle trunk could hug them
or blast bright greetings. *Jumbo*, it rings like
Swahili *jambo*. Perhaps you thought crowds

were being civil, crying out *Hello!*
Why began your rages? Was adolescence
to blame or stress disorder? Has panic
or that cramped stone ghetto made you grind

your tusks to mortar? No, no, Jumbo,
we're giving you human traits. Elephant
sorrow must be bigger than us, cryptic,
as the antelope's soul to the ant.

In the museum we see your bones:
forked at matrix and marrow from chains,
the howdah lifting kids, princes, Churchill.
It's in a docudrama. How Scott your keeper

came to America too, fed you whisky-soaked
biscuits which the zoo claimed would calm
your nightly tantrums. If not,
then spear and hammer would do.

Jumbo, there's a bent wisdom at Barnum's.
In under three years you made him a million.
Now headlines hail you *Spoiled rock star:*
Ashes urned in a peanut butter jar.

How they got there is an odd tale. I'll tell
you, young bush giant, before it's begun.
Still in lush fronds, mother teaches you
water routes, green blankets to blue braids.

How do I teach you *snow?* In the White North
there's a place called Ontario, where flakes
soft as petals fall with metallic chill.
From box cars you'll see this awning plateaus.

Now you're only four. How do I spell out
metal or *train?* Let alone *railway yard.*
Strange terrain Barnum's circus will cross.
That's why Tom Thumb, your wee elephant friend,

will get lost on cold tracks. You'll lead him
from harm when
                              THUD
—but Jumbo, it won't hurt much—

when the train car hits, you'll be whisky-numb.
Whisky is what humans taste for pleasure
or aches. Never tell this part to your mum.
Soon the *Times* will call you *Saviour of Tom*,

and Barnum will have your hide embalmed
and stuffed for a grown-ups' school called Tufts.
Lots of actors have a likeness in wax.
Jumbo, guess what they'll find in your gut?

Keys, pennies, a police whistle. Were they
mixed with your food? Elephant children
should learn: not all things offered are snacks.
Please ask the adults in your herd.

But your aunties don't know what you'll be,
"grown-up." Taxidermied mascot at Tufts.
The sports games' blue romping costume.
You'll enlarge our language. Inspire cartoons.

Clowns will shape you from squeaky balloons.
All air soon, no mass. Your chemical skin
released in Tufts' blaze of 1975,
then scooped up as ash. Look —

all of you now fits in a Skippy jar.
Almost a trick, like when elephants
balance on a tiny ball. Let's pause here.
Go back. Even if weightlessness feels

like freedom — Go back. To jungles. Green.
Learn lightness now, invisibility stunts,
how to vanish from hunters —
                            Go, go, Jumbo,

dissolve into the morass before your trunk
is idolized on big tops and posters.
Your crowd gasps — vanish while the acrobat
wobbles, while the juggler's club drops—

Dark ceilings

Night skies were once syllabified in ballads,
heroes deified in trochaic glints to traipse

through stars. Now there's lambent pollution,
a black lamina glazing the galaxy's mezzanine.

Indoors, a neighbour's floor is our ceiling.
We painted it navy like a sleek magazine—

those photos with polar mood. Dark gloss
we offset by vaulting more watts

until halogen hummed off surplus lumens
and the overhead tenants' pacing was subdued

to dust creeping through cement. We know
someone's home, though we've never met.

In every book we've read that ceilings block
mobility; whether glass or plaster, they crack

when protagonists in stories find secret attics,
laurels, eternity. Against that upstairs-downstairs

tug called gravity, we find new atmospheres in
light suspensions, twisting pictures on screens

with Rubik's-cube utility until we've suspended
a channel—Look, stars on black-hole balconies.

Then we shuffle panoramas to ground-level
digs, cameras troweling ancient rooms.

Our cellars lie on ancestors' roofs, our footprints
sift dirt through sunken ruins, vistas

in old myths packed down by urban planning,
commuters' rushed iambs. Beneath each falling

beat, earth laced with cables, everywhere
scattering radiation and weightless data.

Devonian

Rocks older by zoic-eras, sophomoric and slick
with mosses and molluscs. A climate viscid
with early tetrapods, colossal flora. Strata tempera,
when insects innovated slowly in Gondwana,
when amphibian yolks in Euramerica puddled
in backwaters; little gold auras becoming tadpoles
with a stroke, chromatic flecks in the billions-big biota.

Small fauna, relics glassed in exhibits. Crushed
by calcite or resin-gummed, skeletons that experts
gesso with muscle. Scales and tones guessed
by palaeontologists, chiming with dyes in art rooms
nearby. Pedantic plaques suggest Devonian palettes
were narrow, when oceans lassoed land, impassable,
and flashiness was risky in the greater hunger.

Perhaps. Shrouded by fronds, proto-chameleons
mingled in malachite mattes, or varnished their backs
to fascinate mates, cloning an indigo spectrum,
spawning thousandfold replicas. Museum-goers
are titillated by halos of rust and rarity, the crumble
of a mother-and-child. Brushes that recovered ancient
bodies, icons once so common one might string
their slight bones on a rosary.

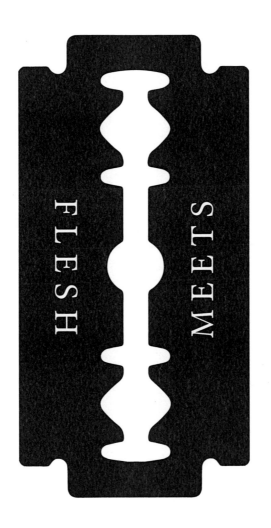

In the Uffizi Gallery on our honeymoon

Rooms budding with Annunciations:
Virgin fringed with emblems of myrtle
and lily, sheltered in a portico

when Gabriel alights. Pregnancy
heralded by a textband stretching
from the angel's mouth, or lightrays

striking her from the Spirit in the corner.
Here's something new, we say, glued
in a sea of devotees, *The Birth of Venus*.

But look, I say, *this scene's another
Annunciation*: Venus touched
by the gust from Zephyr's lips, circled

by flowers and her cockle porch.
Hora offers royal robes to clothe her
in modesty. Today's an exposé.

We float out to the Piazza.
The Palazzo palms me in its crenellated
conch. The wind cinches my waist, says,

You're naked; says, *I'm handing you flowers.*
You buy me roses from a sharp-eyed vendor.
We're moved by gods, I know it.

Today our mise-en-scene is faultless.
Let me enjoy it. For decades I floated
alone in a little shell, saving it

from splitting with backbone and grit.
You didn't blow in on an announcement,
never rescued me from swells I couldn't handle.

But when we met at eye-level I knew
I was blessed, stepping off a rough-brushed
ocean, sure of the story, not even wet.

Oral tradition

On bright screens I compare facsimiles
of old ballads, vellum's finials and minims
telling a folktale's strayed endings.

In text A, a village toasts strangers
with hot wine, soft rhymes. In B, with blood
from slaughters, trading gold for daughters.

Do variations complete each other,
or vie for authenticity? I quiz you
over dinner, the day's research pending

type, its gothic glyphs and stock phrases.
We extemporize on transmission, how
oral lore morphs before it's pinioned to script.

What do you remember the night we met?
That September we volunteered
at the shelter, talked medieval lit

while scrubbing floors. If I scribed it,
you quoted Ronsard and knocked over
a bucket. If you did, I untangled

kennings and hefted too much rubbish.
We knew then we'd marry,
though we've edited our first brags

and blunders. Two years before we met
again, before we sipped sweet wine
instead of lukewarm blood.

What story doesn't mourn lost time?
There's no best text of our shared traditions,
no rubric for trimming aberrations.

Your cursive bleeds through my blackletter.
I'll drink to that.
If we're coupled in our memoirs' close,

let facts lapse in copies we render, let
tongues helix the tellings 'til cloistered
hands write our endings cruel or tender.

"Dying well"

Warriors collude to kill me,
birches brandishing wound-branches.
Why not face time's last small space
secure? Everyone dies. Iron-brands
roast my bones and marrow. Remember,
lady, a hero's heart was forged for me.
Poetry is my tool in tough times.
It pays tribute to my grit.

End replication problem

Thin caps bandage our DNA, this morning's
news explains. Chromosomes only replicate
in the middle. With each division, telomeres
shrivel until the unclothed genome dies.

It's before seven, and I'm unsettled by the
end replication problem. At the molecular
level, stress shortens lifespan. A tough job
claws at our nucleotide's fine gauze.

Even *sitting too long wears down this cushion.*
You've been at work since dawn, shoulders
hunched toward attrition, cortisol rippling in
analog waves. The antidote is a bandaid hour:

*Walk at lunch. Get sun. Eat greens that won't
raise insulin.* Your break lasts thirty minutes,
darting through downpour for a wilted sandwich
in plastic adhesive, to devour at the office.

Waiting at traffic corners for electric men
to flip to ticking hands, the membrane
of your umbrella shielding you from drizzle,
its tissue puckering in the dash to beat zeros.

At your door, spokes resist closing, metal
elbows now decrepit, knocking seconds off
schedules. This is your remedy, what you clutch
adrenal from deadlines shredding the day.

My love, how will these pinched minutes delay
the ends' unfastening? Your hour is not a crutch
prolonging life's reach, its final split and hobble.
It's where you break apart from nothing much.

Hydro hookup

Our home slept unwired.

You woke pumps to well-water, cedars to fire.

I made stew on hobs sissing gold and blue.

Those first years, no void ambered within the glue of atoms.

We worked together, reading by solar-dull bulbs, mining
    supplies from peel and pulp.

But we never lived subsistence, without chucking tannic skins,
    without candling info from rogue signals.

Phones palmed outwards, we divined on hillocks, found cellular
    nectar that taught us to caulk windows, uncrystal honey.

Was there a dry spell before Hydro?

Before its truck — heavy, yellow —came bombing into bedrock,
    bringing our ounce of data.

Now we tap tap flat buttons, sip video, pass each other
    squinting over its effervescent glow.

The lamps are too gold.

With a touch to any switch, moths flock, their parched wings
    drawn by paradox to fluorescence and heat.

We mined and found a new element and it's dry.

Its tiny chevrons have unchained themselves from wires, settled
    over our cabin humming non sync.

If I could cup this power and release it outside —but in palms it
    is less than dust.

I miss the green and gold in your eyes.

Awake with you across time zones

This pale, two-day moon
has not found your shore. Lidless,
my wandering eye.

First flood

That evening a solvent, everything finishing in blue: garden, hemlocks, the metal-on-bone rake you swung to tissue earth. Evening like floods rising, a lake lapping glass. From the room behind my shoulder, the apricot lamp spotted the pane. Moon climbing too early over water.

For dinner, you prepared wineless bread. An egg over-boiled until its yolk crumbled. Bowls swelled from the table like unfilled bellies. Spoons scooped arid roots, the day's thirst. Knives scraped, saw-toothed, recalling chair legs without casters, scarring the hush from the stethoscope.

Before the blood, we dug tubers from the garden, but my palms tore on shapes harder. *These bones are my mother's. If we throw them over our shoulders we'll re-seed the soil.* But when you raked the earth again, they were stones. I heard you whisper thinly, as though to broken pottery in the cupboard, *New life won't grow where you grew.*

To bed

We've budded a sweet pea with webbed hands
and feet, heart beating double-time at six weeks.
Has she yet seen the black-and-white figures
in dreams, pulled the anchor of her blood-bed
for release? How long will she rest in me?
Until the snap of a broken trisomy?
Or will we tuck her into a trundle,
find too soon she's sailed in a wooden shoe
on crystal light, seas of dew? An old moon
asks her "Where are you going?" and by his
dim bloom leads her to another perch.
We saw it on the ultrasound's dark squares:
yolk-sac waning, ballooned above her reaching
limbs. At this point, fear and hope both slim.

20-week scan

We saw you through bounced sound,
organs and tissue outlined
echogenic, black space to bright curve.

Ten inches without muscle, lips
parted to swallow amnion.
We searched you for anomalies,

shrill hertz bombarding your skeleton
as you curled into a ball, dodging
the transducer's hot pressure.

To your unborn ear, what noise funnels?
My body dulls this concrete world
by half, but inside's a jungle:

heart thump, blood pump, hips popping
unstiff as my feet hit pavement,
molars grinding, sniff-sniff. My voice?

A muted jet engine, the airplane's hum
to passengers snug in aluminum.
They say humans can't hear ultrasound

frequencies, but kids catch higher pitch.
From the white noise machine of mother's
body, we're a species programmed to listen

with distance, adoring oceans remote
in a conch, rain pattering on roofs,
background music, soothing crackle

of logs on looped TV channels.
On these tones your father and I coast
through winter, forego foreign travel,

speak of you. His bass caroms images,
half accurate perhaps. After the first
made-up years, our words static back

until we're parent ships projecting signals,
hoping you'll echo. The bigger you grow,
the less we know you've heard us

our sonar broken
on open ocean

Labour, Eastertime 2019

How long does a resurrection take?
Experts debate: three days
by calendar or sleeps.

Three days from first timed pains
to birth, to rising and beholding you
at the tubes' removal.

We lost count of hours without an epidural,
hoping for *natural* — cervix dilating idly
like a thin new moon.

Narrow pelvis, obstructed head. Mouths shrouded
in blue plastic. Wrists, ankles starfished
to the OR table. I didn't eat for two days,

I promised. Only Jello in a flavour
rainbow improbable to vomit.
Viscera offered so empty to blades.

A friend visits the hospital, coos at our son's
long eyelashes before spilling acid:
A C-section isn't giving birth.

Oh my son, from where did you come?
It's true I didn't see you until the curtain
lifted. But other hands are always first

to catch, pull, hold you. Alone
I feed you, while the postnatal
room's analog snips through sleep.

Every three hours from the body to eat.
At home, we tally input/output
on our phones, learn hunger cues.

Each gained ounce balanced
with a calcium tablet. Nursing you is hunger
to cup your acorn-small shoulder, crook

your unknit skull. How often I explain:
no stitches hold my kindled skin together,
                              just glue.

Supernatural fluid. Yet the birth
stories we honour end with mother's
rent lips, not polymered tissue.

If not for these cuttings, I wouldn't hold you,
your skin fine-spun on my raw tummy.
Surely, to be saved at birth is holy.

What happened to the temple veil after
spirit burned through? Discarded, no longer
fit for use? or salvaged and remade —

warmer, cushion, bed,
red seams covenanting bandaged flesh,
this shabby world where you cry out to rest.

Helicopter Father

Our toddler unlatches doors so fast, crying
Out, out. His playground is beyond his father's
house, his mother's floors swept clean of risk.

Safety-tested gifts he shuns for mud and sticks,
oozing slugs, the surf's tickling suck.
We know each wonder is toy and hazard —

pulse-tripping foxgloves,
berry-dotted dropoffs,
barnacle's razors.

There is a myth of immanence,
that a father's eye sees every harm
as it's inflicted —

for it's written, the universe is planted
in innocence and sin.
Our son's garden is endless.

Eden, maybe, was baby-proof,
no roots to trip small feet, no puddle
too deep, no plum-pits to eat.

Eve would lay Abel on pillowed soil, turn
her back to pick apples. Adam would teach
Cain to name a crèche of hungry tigers.

But God peered into his play-yard and spied
the danger. He cried *Out, out*
to any would-be toddlers.

Then angels' sword-flames slashed round
like chopper blades to save this sheltered
space from unborn babes.

"Áslaug's three sorrows"

I.
Shabby shifts best fit my
figure. This silver-stranded dress
I don't dare receive, well worn
by that woman Þóra the Hart.
I am called The Crow
because I've combed sea-crags
wearing coal-dark cloaks,
driving goats by the deep.

II.
Husband, let's not make love these
first three nights, but spend hours
high-spirited in our hall before
we sacrifice to the holy gods.
Even so, I see my son, his pain
prolonged. Ragnarr, you're rash
in the face of my prophecy,
quick to beget a boneless boy.

III.
My sons, you left me too long
wave-watching at the seagull's-ground.
What were you up to? Surely not
paying visits house to house?
Now you let loose this news: my son
Rǫgnvaldr reddened his shield
with men's gore; your blood-brother
then went battle-bold to Óðinn's hall.

Heirlooms

*After a painting by Jack Humphries, of a crumbling mansion in
New Brunswick*

Canadian romantic: a sagging mansion
in the Kennebecasis, its pastel
lintels throttled by pines.

Few visit the canvas in Ottawa's vaults.
Thin, this tribute to my mother's family, the home
great-grandfather abandoned in the Depression.

A mill-mogul who gave the poor all his silks
and silver, 'till his sons milked cows,
played hooky in split shoes.

As a teen grandad grudged charity, tracked down false
heirs and begged his legacy. Said he learned
about dogs and their owners.

I could go to Ottawa. Claim my lost bone,
though I wasn't the donor. What else can I give my sons
from my mother but pale eyes and stories?

The last trinkets went to aunts, pregnant mice
in basements. To covet is sin. I've sat through sermons.
But no preacher names this greed to hoard

for my children. There's a dream I have, where I guide
my tiny sons through a house of many rooms, find
dead kin in cameos beside burnished heirlooms.

I say, *All this was prepared by your Father.*
They ignore lessons, crayon walls,
find rodent bones in vases.

Bullets

Gardens lapsed to alders, castoff rakes.
Shed sagging, parched of paint. Around this
backwoods house, traps accumulate.
Weeds rope the steps and the door's warped,
bolts leadened like arthritic joints.
Cold. Both air and floors. Rugs bunched
with ankle-level cords. Even corners, damp
and whipslick tiled. Bulbs snap to shrapnel
in halls, conscripting brooms and ladders;
steel rungs slung against gravity.
The voice mail trills point-blank; a cartridge
storing angst in garbled catalogues.
Isolation is a gun old hands load, then pull
by basement stairs, forgotten stoves.

Biometrics

Bifocal lines brushed through window vapour where
you checked the weather. How I slept through your
morning dues—the light switch finds jars and handles
autographed with butter, stainless steel fingertipped
deceitful before you backdoored yourself to mist.

Some prints rinse, water-cloaked, the bar soap sunken
from your clutch fluxing wafer-thin. On limbs, castile
sudsing away night and lust's nucleic chafe. How I've
rubbed the fogged mirror, face vised in its zero-zero
axis, and mothed my glasses with an index finger.

Cataracts glove our home, opaque spots haunting
what you've touched. So much is chromosomed
and overlapped, firewood we stacked with brittle skin,
the blood clues burned to sap. My hands arc chore-worn,
chapped, won't blur furniture with oil, won't anoint

corners on your eroded books. Too long you've circled
home on errands; hard to map fingerprints, dust cups
idling on tables. With bifocals I'm a forensic cop,
observing things too far and too close up.

On windows I find your initials, through skimmed film
see woodsmoke paranormal the forest like arms and torso.

"Old age"

Blind I bumbled to the fire,
courting kindness from a fighting
lady, woman of the spear
of war-falcons, wanting to rest there.
My eyelids haul such hardship.
Long ago, a land-rich king
relished my poetry,
loaded me with hero's weapons.

I lie long hours.
To me at least.
A broken-down old guy
far from the king's vanguard.
I still own two widows,
two frozen legs,
but those ladies hanker
for furnace-heat.

Four drawers

Objects were entrusted to you, but you were a magician's box;
in cryptic pockets wadding socks and tops. Refusing to shut
flush, lips jut. In sullen summers you will not open, rollers
swollen. When clocks fall back and barometers drop, your
knobs will be pumped; varathane shrilling on ruts.

Not dualistic like mind-body tropes, your oak hutches thewed
to swaddle clothes and memorabilia, yielding musty ghosts. I
came upon you outcast, no-cost. Dead-lifted and trucked off
a burnished lawn. I ransomed you with an artisan's aplomb;
fancying my hands could saw smashed stuff modish, or torch
defectives, petrol-apathetic.

Free-cycled. So much I own and know from other homes
and frontal lobes. Now things turncoat when I coax them
towards purposes, try to out-trivia folks. Instinct and mimesis
once found me gratis, a tabula rasa. These days I'm drawn to
drawers, spatial metaphors; the switch where panels flip up
learning crypts, hocussed hollows.

There's an estival-autumnal tumble. Some say, gnashing on
brimstone follows, or ashes whisked through the blue. Others
see their souls re-teething, growing fossilized knowledge in
new cartilage. My mind stalls in a carnal garage, where lost
scraps can be collared. A body in a boneyard, shut too hard.

If time devours

by now its belly must bloat.

We read of cities clogged with poverty.
Scarcity driving scavenger teeth
to landfills. Artifacts cramped into
earth-organs. Edifices and bones grown
acid-rain porous. Time burns fuels
and forests, sucks glaciers like ice cubes.

Time scours our house too, poaching
morsels on mice-feet, coughing dust
balls and staling pantry staples. Joints
crack when we cook or sweep. Most hours,
we ward off falls, keep to chairs, swap
books or facts. The universe is a seamless sack,

contours straining with solids and gasses.
Star-disks fizzle, like alka-seltzer tablets
dropped in water glasses. For years we've
chewed news with mechanical grace,
appetite gone with sense of taste.
After supper, we drain shots of pH.

Baskets

Take the wastepaper basket, palm fronds woven
to hold tissues, last weeks' reminders for Razadyne.
Take clothes, bird ornaments, until we've cleared
the Annex, where all are nursed through rooms quickly,
plied from bleached blankets. Take memory, a sediment
sieved to us daughters from impurities and stardust's
energy. All baskets are made to empty.
Watch. Down the church aisle floats an illusion
box, hiding form from spellbound mourners
through a glitter of readings. Arms too spent
for this service. We've nudged knick-knacks from shelves,
counted prayer pamphlets, but no one's ready for this
open lid—*Holy, holy the Lord God Almighty*—
why do we preserve what we'll bury?

Notes & Acknowledgements

Some of the poems in this manuscript are my translations of Old Norse-Icelandic skaldic verse: "Auðr mourns her dead brother" are verses by Gísli Súrsson (10th Century); "Sonatorrek" ("Loss of Sons") is a selection of verses from a long poem by Egill Skallagrímsson (10th Century); "Rune carving" and "Old age" are also from Skallagrímsson's work; "Verse-making" is from a fragment by Hallar-Steinn (12th Century); "Áslaug's three sorrows" are translations of three verses attributed to the legendary figure Áslaug Sigurðardóttir, appearing within the prose of the 13th-century saga, *Ragnars saga loðbrókar*, and "Dying well" is from a verse by Gísl Illugason (11th Century).

Some of these poems have appeared in previous publications, and have won or been shortlisted for prizes. Thanks to the editors who believed in these poems: "Venn diagrams" won *The Malahat Review*'s Far Horizons Award for Poetry 2018 and was first published in *The Malahat Review* Issue 204; "Glassblowing" won an honourable mention in CV2's Foster Poetry Prize (2018) and was first published in CV2 Vol. 41, Issue 1; "Brute facts" won Runner-up in *Eyewear Review*'s inaugural Fortnight Prize 2017; "Biometrics" was long-listed for *The Puritan*'s Thomas Morton Prize for Poetry 2017; "End replication problem" was first published in *Vallum* 17:2; "If time devours" and "Dark ceilings" were first published in *The Malahat Review* Issue 206; "First flood" was first published in *Canthius* Issue 5; "Diacritics" was first published in *Minola Review* Issue 16; "Sharp parables" was first published in *Barren Magazine* Issue 3; "Bullets" was first published in *The Antigonish Review* Issue 193; "Devonian" was first published in *PULP Literature* Issue 17. Several of these poems also appeared in the chapbook *Biometrical* (Anstruther Press, 2018), which I am grateful to Jim Johnstone for publishing.

Gratitude is difficult to package. Daniel: thank you always for urging me to write again after a long pause, for being a brilliant critic, and for filling our small home with countless books. Thank you to friends from my Vancouver and Bowen Island writing groups, who offered sage advice on drafts of many of these poems: Charlene Kwiatkowski, Diane Tucker, Jolene Nolte, Sheila Rosen, Michael Penny, and Susan Alexander. Thank you to Rahat Kurd for conversations on writing and translation. Thank you to my mother, Mary, for the writing gene and encouraging me as a child. Thanks to Shane Neilson for reaching out and believing in my work, when I thought I could never get a manuscript out the door.

About the Author

Emily Osborne's poetry, short fiction and Old Norse-to-English verse translations have appeared in numerous journals and anthologies. She is the author of the poetry chapbook *Biometrical* (Anstruther Press). In 2018, Emily won *The Malahat Review*'s Far Horizons Award for Poetry and received an honourable mention in *CV2*'s Foster Poetry Prize. Emily completed an MPhil and PhD at the University of Cambridge, in Old English and Old Norse Literature. Currently, she lives on Bowen Island, BC, with her husband and two young sons.

Safety Razor is her debut book of poetry.